GEORGE GERSHWIN

RHAPSODY IN BLUE

2 PIANOS, 4 HANDS

Edited by Bre

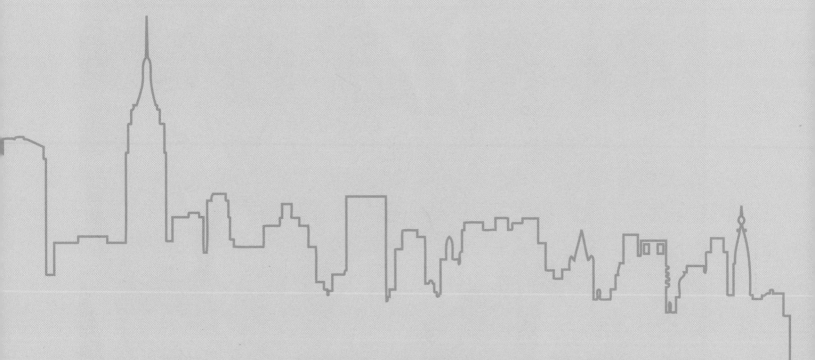

ISBN 978-1-5400-4027-5

HAL•LEONARD®

Visit Hal Leonard Online at
www.halleonard.com

Contact us:
Hal Leonard
7777 West Bluemound Road
Milwaukee, WI 53213
Email: info@halleonard.com

In Europe, contact:
Hal Leonard Europe Limited
42 Wigmore Street
Marylebone, London, W1U 2RN
Email: info@halleonardeurope.com

In Australia, contact:
Hal Leonard Australia Pty. Ltd.
4 Lentara Court
Cheltenham, Victoria, 3192 Australia
Email: info@halleonard.com.au

Gershwin in 1924.
(Photo by Hulton Archive/Getty Images)

CONTENTS

PREFACE

For some people, *Rhapsody in Blue* is a delectable slice of concert jazz. For others, it is inextricable from its setting as a soundtrack in *Fantasia 2000*. For others, the piece is a symbol of New York City or America itself. Its 1924 premiere performance at a concert titled "An Experiment in Modern Music" represented a fortunate collision of artists at the right time. Gershwin was becoming established as a theatre composer but had some inclinations toward art music. Paul Whiteman, leader of the wildly popular Palais Royal Orchestra, wanted a concert hall performance that would further legitimize his band, and to "make an honest woman out of jazz," in the words of his contemporaries. And Ferde Grofé, one of Whiteman's choice arrangers, brought his particular skill to orchestrating Gershwin's music with the unique instrumental colors of Whiteman's ensemble.

The editorial process for this edition involved studying all available published editions of the two-piano reduction and the full score, Gershwin's original recordings, and every *Rhapsody in Blue* source from the George and Ira Gershwin Collection at the Library of Congress. Sources were compared, with all relevant findings detailed in the Notes section.

One point gleaned from this research was that in the earliest years of its history, the Rhapsody's form was somewhat malleable. Gershwin's earliest two-piano manuscript includes several passages for piano solo that were subsequently removed (notated in pages 12–15 in the Notes). The two earliest recordings of the piece also omit large sections, likely to accommodate the time limits of early recording formats. These recordings clock in at just under nine minutes, compared to the standard concert length of about eighteen. And even the Warner Brothers edition of the two-piano reduction bears a footnote about optional cuts in the music.

The comparison of sources also raised the issue of articulation. Ferde Grofé's orchestration gives far more articulation and specific dynamics than are indicated in the long-standing piano reduction. To document all of these details, even in editorial brackets, would be to travel down a rabbit hole, and likely counterproductive. The lack of certain details in the reduction points to its purpose as an accompaniment, and to the piano's difference in sound production compared to a solo trumpet or clarinet. But two spots merited an editorial addition of dynamics. In m. 127, the orchestra has a *tutti* passage marked *ff* in both of the full score sources, but no dynamic was ever given in the two-piano reduction. We applied a *ff* mark in brackets for the orchestra and *f* for the solo piano. Then in mm. 200–202 and 204–206, the piano has no articulation in a passage that repeats heavily articulated material from mm. 181–188. It seemed appropriate to include the earlier articulations as an optional guide.

Special thanks to Chamisa Redmond and Robert Lipartito at the Library of Congress for their help and insight, and to Richard Walters for editorial consultation.

Brendan Fox, editor
December 2019

SOURCES CONSULTED

M   George Gershwin's holograph manuscript for piano and jazz band (Jazz band reduced for second piano). January 1, 1924. George and Ira Gershwin Collection, 1895–2008. Library of Congress. Washington, D.C. This manuscript source is missing lots of articulation, dynamics, tempo, etc. and contains several passages of piano solo material that do not appear any other source. In some instances the solo piano part is entirely blank, or with a shorthand to be filled in later.

T   Ferde Grofé's holograph manuscript for solo piano and jazz band. February 4, 1924. "Rhapsody in Blue: Commemorative Facsimile Edition." Alfred Publishing Co, Inc, 1987. Similar to **M**, some sections leave the piano part blank, or with a shorthand to be filled in later.

J   Bound, printed score for piano and jazz band (band part reduced for second piano). Harms, Inc., 1924. George and Ira Gershwin Collection, 1895–2008. Library of Congress. Washington, D.C. This first published edition established the form of the piece for performance, but many details were changed or added for **W**.

G   George Gershwin's facsimile copy of Grofé's symphonic orchestration. February 23, 1926. George and Ira Gershwin Collection, 1895–2008. Library of Congress. Washington, D.C.

S   Miniature score of Grofé's symphonic orchestration. Alfred Publishing Co., Inc, 1942. This represents the full-orchestra version commonly played in concerts today, with a few minor differences in the piano part compared to **W**.

W   Bound, printed two-piano edition. Warner Brothers Music Corporation, 1924. This source adds many articulations, dynamics, and tempo markings that are not present in **J**. It has remained, for decades, the primary performance edition of the piece.

R^I   Acoustic recording with Paul Whiteman Orchestra, conducted by Paul Whiteman. Gershwin as pianist. June 10, 1924. Abridged; duration is 8:59. Cuts are specified in the Notes.

R^{II}   Electrical recording with Paul Whiteman Orchestra, conducted by Nathaniel Shilkret. Gershwin as pianist. April 21, 1927. Abridged; duration is 9:01. Cuts are specified in the Notes.

Also consulted:

The Annotated Rhapsody in Blue. Alicia Zizzo, editor. Alfred Publishing Co, Inc, 1996.

George Gershwin: His Life and Work. Howard Pollack. University of California Press, 2006.

NOTES

The 1924 Warner Bros. two-piano edition (**W**) was our primary source.
Comments about details from other sources which differ from **W** follow below.

SECTION I: SOLO PIANO PART

m. 19, **M**, **T**: *f* dynamic for both hands. **G**, **S**: *mf* for both hands; crescendo hairpin on beats 3–4.

mm. 21–23, **M**: key signature of G-flat major.

m. 21, **J**: *energico*, no tempo head of **Più mosso**. **M**, **T**: different chords on beat 4 (see below).

m. 22, **J**, **G**: no accents on first chord in R.H. and L.H.

mm. 22–23, **M**, **T**:

m. 23, **M**: bottom note of the fourth L.H. chord is D-flat. **J**: second note of beat 3 is D-double-flat. **G**: second note of beat 3 is E with no natural sign.

m. 24, **G**, **S**: no *poco scherzando*. **J**: no flats on R.H. chord; probably a mistake.

mm. 24–27, **M**: different phrasing and articulation.

mm. 25–26, **S**: slurs in both hands end on last note of m. 25, beat 4.

m. 29, **J**: no *dim*.

m. 32, **M**: no dynamics.

m. 33, **S**: L.H. mark on beat 1.

mm. 33–34, **M**: no dynamics, accents instead of martellato marks.

mm. 34–35, **S**: triplets written out. The two-piano reductions (**W**, **J**, and **M**) use shorthand.

m. 37, **M**: no crescendo.

m. 39, **G**: no second pair of hairpins on beats 3–4.

mm. 41–42, **M**: bottom note of L.H. chords through m. 42, beat 2 is A. Later sources have G-natural.

mm. 42, 47, **G, J**: no *poco rit.* on beat 4. In **G**, the *poco rit.* is notated for the ochestra.

mm. 46–47, **M**: bottom note of all L.H. chords is A. Later sources have G-natural.

m. 48, **G**: **Tranquillo** as a tempo head instead of an expression.

mm. 55–56, 58–60, **M**: different phrasing and articulation.

mm. 66–67, **M**, **J**, **R^{I}**, **R^{II}**: no L.H. notes on downbeats.

m. 66, **G**: last L.H. note is F instead of E in other sources.

m. 71, **G**: slurs on last 3 notes in R.H. instead of last 4. **M, T**: slur over each beat.

m. 77, **M**: chords in both hands are quarter notes instead of eighths.

m. 85, **J**: no dynamic.

m. 87, **J**: accent on first R.H. chord.

m. 90, **J**: no staccato on R.H. chord.

m. 103, **J**: 8va begins here instead of in m. 102.

m. 106, **M**: note on piano part: "continue 1 more bar," implying a continuation of the arpeggio sequence from m. 105.

m. 109, **J:** no dynamic on beat 1.

m. 114, **T**: piano doubles orchestra on beat 4.

m. 127, **M**: "octaves" written above the piano staff.

mm. 146–152, **M**: "Gliss" written at m. 146, with a shorthand line continuing through m. 152. There are no clues as to what Gershwin meant by this.

m. 165, **J**: no "*loco*" text on second note.

m. 192, **J**: no martellato mark on beat 1.

m. 195, **S**, **G**: slur from last R.H. note into m. 196. **J**: last L.H chord is an 8th, not a 16th, with no fermata. No *rit.* mark on beat 2.

m. 198, **G**, **S**: R.H. slur starts on second note instead of first.

mm. 200–202, 204–206, **S**: articulation in R.H. not present in **W**. These articulations match the similar passage in mm. 181–188, and have been notated in brackets.

m. 203, **J**: "*R.H. ad lib.*" on beat 4 instead of "*R.H.*"

m. 208, **S**: no accent in L.H., beat 1.

mm. 209, 211, **J**: no martellato on beat 1.

m. 214–219, **J**: no arpeggio marks on L.H. chords.

m. 215, 219, **J**: no tie from beat 2 to 3 in the R.H.

m. 216, **J**: grace note on beat 3 is B, not D.

m. 217, **G**, **J**: 8th-note E on beat 2 instead of a tied D.

m. 224, **J**: no tie from beat 2 to 3 in the L.H.

m. 225, **M**: sharp symbol in the L.H. is on the line for D, though there is no D in the chord; probably intended for the F in the chord as in subsequent sources.

m. 227, **M**: L.H. chord on beat 3 is a half note. Triplets on beat 4 are instrumental cues.

m. 244, **J**: staccato on F in the R.H., beat 2.

m. 256, **S**: no dynamic marking.

m. 297, **J**: 8va starts one beat earlier than **G**, **S**, and **W**; probably a mistake.

m. 327, **J**: dynamic p instead of f in **W**.

m. 328, **G**: decrescendo hairpin on beats 2–4.

m. 336, **G**: crescendo hairpin on beats 2–4.

m. 337, **J**: dynamic f instead of ff in **W**.

mm. 343–346, **M**, **T**: last chords of mm. 343 and 345 tied into next measure as an 8th note.

mm. 357–358, 365–366, **J**: no slurs in R.H.

m. 371, **J**: no **mf** dynamic or *espr.* marking.

mm. 373–374, **J**: no accents in R.H.

m. 378, **R**[I]: Gershwin plays the last two notes in the R.H. as 8ths rather than 16ths, starting on beat 4. **T**: R.H. ends with 8th-note E instead of two 16ths.

m. 384, **J**, **S**: staccato marking.

m. 387, **J**: instruction in **W** "(start slowly and gradually increase to speed)" not present.

m. 410, **M**: the final E is a sixteenth note and followed by a sixteenth G-sharp.

m. 425, **J**: no dynamic.

m. 433, **J**: no dynamic.

mm. 437, 439, **J**: no sharp on D in R.H.

m. 451, **J**, **W**: **ff**, probably a mistake.

mm. 465–466, **J**: top note of L.H. chords is G-double-sharp, probably a mistake.

mm. 504–505, **G**, **S**: piano doubles orchestra on beat 4 leading into beat 1 of m. 505.

m. 505, **S**: no arpeggio marking in L.H, beat 3.

mm. 505–507, **J**: piano part is different from any other source.

m. 506, **G**, **S**: grace notes in L.H., beats 1–2.

m. 507, **S**: arpeggio marking in L.H., beat 2.

m. 508, **M**, **J**: octaves in R.H. instead of full chords.

m. 510, **J**: staccato markings in both hands.

SECTION II: ORCHESTRA PART

m. 6, **R¹**: the clarinet plays this trill with A-natural as the upper note.

mm. 6, 8, **M**: staccato markings on second note of beats 2–4.

m. 10, **R¹ R¹¹**, **S**: flat trill, common performance practice, applied in this edition.

mm. 11–13, **M**: staccato markings on second 8th note of each slurred pair.

m. 15, **M**: no flats on the A and D-flat of the 10-tuplet.

m. 16, **R¹**, **R¹¹**: no grace notes on beat 3 of the trumpet part (R.H. in piano reduction). **M, G, S**: accent instead of staccato on beat 3.

m. 18, **M**: staccato instead of tenuto in R.H., beat 2.

mm. 26–29, **R¹**, **R¹¹**: orchestra doubles piano melody. Not reflected in any printed source.

mm. 72, 77, **J**: tenutos instead of accents on downbeat of beats 3 and 4.

m. 80, **M**: no bass line in L.H.

m. 82: **J**, **W**: staccato mark on the C instead of the D, inconsistent with mm. 81 and 83. Edited to make slurring and articulation consistent in mm. 81–83.

m. 85, **J**: *mf* instead of *f* in orchestra part. **G, S**: accents in the entire orchestra that would make up L.H. beats 2 and 4, and the first notes in the R.H. beats 3–4.

m. 107, **M**: R.H., beat 3 is two 8ths, B-flat to A-flat.

m. 108, **M**: R.H., beats 1 and 3 are two 8th notes, A-flat to B-flat and B-flat to C-sharp, respectively.

m. 111, **M**: R.H., beat 3 is two 8ths, G to F.

m. 112, **M**: R.H., beats 1 and 3 are two 8ths, F to G and G to A-sharp, respectively.

m. 117, **J**: no accent or slur on last R.H. chord.

mm. 121–123, **J**: starting m. 121, beat 4, no accents or slur. Second L.H. octave in m. 122 is not tied.

mm. 125–127, **G, S**: orchestra has a dynamic mark on each bar. In order: *mf*, *p*, *ff*. Of these, the *ff* in m. 127 is standard performance practice and has been added in brackets for this edition, along with *f* for the solo piano for balance.

m. 130, **G, S**: *con licenza*.

mm. 134–135, **M, T, J**: *ritard* starts in m. 135.

m. 137, **J**: L.H. has low D octave on beat 4 and no fermata.

mm. 138–140, 142–144, 146–151, **M**: text "Perhaps" with another rhythm for orchestra's accompanying chords written on a separate staff above m. 138. **G**, **S**: rhythm from **M** is notated in the flutes and clarinets in the bars mentioned in this note.

m. 139, **G**, **S**: entire orchestra has an accent on F in L.H., beat 1.

m. 140, **S**: orchestra has accents instead of tenutos on the triplet.

m. 151, **J**: no accents on C and B-flat in L.H.

m. 152, **J**: no *mf* and *rit.* marks.

m. 153, **J**: *ritard.* here instead of in m. 153 as in **W** and **S**.

mm. 155, 157, **G**: accents on every melody note in both hands.

m. 157, **J**, **W**: the first R.H. chord has no notehead for A-flat, probably a mistake.

mm. 158–165, **G**: accents on offbeat 8ths in L.H. in addition to the downbeats.

mm. 159, 164, **G**, **S**: accents instead of tenutos on the triplet.

m. 169, **J**: no accent on last L.H. note.

m. 170, **J**: no dynamic on beat 1.

mm. 200–206, **M**: no tenutos. Slurs over each 2-bar phrase of the horn part. In mm. 204–206, **G** has tenutos on each note.

mm. 212–213, **M**: no tenutos. Slurs over each 2-bar phrase of the horn part. In m. 213, **S** has a tenuto on the first note and the slur begins on beat 3 instead of beat 1.

m. 238, **J**, **G**: no flat on whole-note C in R.H. We believe the addition of a flat in **W** was a mistake, and have removed it.

mm. 305–310, 313–316, **G**, **S**: accents on first note of horn part which forms the moving line.

mm. 327–332, **G**, **S**: accents on first note of trumpet part which forms the moving line.

m. 313, **J**: no crescendo hairpin.

mm. 313–316, **M**: cue-size chords added in L.H.: E3 to C-sharp 4 tied in mm. 313–314, E-sharp 3 to C-sharp 4 tied in m. 315–316.

m. 315, **J**, **W**: no tie on bottom B in R.H., probably a mistake.

m. 317, **J**: no dynamic.

m. 318, **M**: on second R.H. chord, E added as second note from the bottom.

m. 319, **J**: no slur on first three R.H. chords. **M**: third R.H. chord has no B, adds E as second note from the bottom.

m. 320, **J**: no decrescendo.

m. 321, **J**: no *rit.*

mm. 323–324, **J**: *rit.* and crescendo from m. 323, beat 2 to m. 324, beat 2. **W**: no *rit.*, crescendo starts m. 324, beat 3.

m. 326, **J**: no accents.

mm. 343–346, **G**, **S**: staccato on every note. Strings in this passage are playing pizzicato.

m. 425, **J**: *p* instead of *mf*. **M**, **G**, **S**: accents on first and last notes.

m. 429, **M**, **G**, **S**: accents on first and last notes.

m. 433, **J**: no dynamic.

m. 440, **G, S**: on triplet notes in beat 4, *fz* instead of accents.

mm. 443–447, **J**: "*tremolo ad lib,*" tremolos not written out.

mm. 467–470, **G, S**: accent on each chord; *poco a poco crescendo* starting at m. 467. **T**: crescendo at m. 467.

mm. 471–472, **G**: *fz* on beat 2.

m. 486, **M**: last four notes in both hands notated as 16ths, corrected to 32nds in **W**.

mm. 487–496, 501–502, **G**: accents on all offbeat 8th notes.

m. 504, **G**, **S**: *f*, accent on each note of the triplet, crescendo on beat 4.

m. 505, **G**: low F continues in triplet chords in beats 3–4.

m. 509, **M**, **G**: crescendo.

m. 510, **J**: staccato in both hands. **G**: *ffz*.

SECTION III: FORM AND TEMPO ISSUES
IMPACTING BOTH PIANO AND ORCHESTRA

Cuts taken on recordings may have been due to time limitations of the recording formats.

The footnote about optional cuts appears in **J**, **G**, **S**, and **W**. Preserved here for practical applications.

m. 113, **J**: "*rall.*"; **W** has "*rall. e dim.*"

m. 115, **J**: "a tempo."

m. 137, **R**^{I}, **R**^{II}: cut from here to m. 170.

m. 155, **T**: 4 additional bars in score, a near-repeat of material in mm. 138–141.

m. 193, **M**: 7 additional bars in piano solo. Passage crossed out on manuscript, whether by Gershwin or someone else.

m. 195, **R**^{I}, **R**^{II}: cut from here to m. 299.

m. 222, **M**: 10 additional bars in piano solo.

m. 228, **J**: no tempo.

mm. 297–302, **T**: these bars of the cadenza not present.

m. 303, **J**: no "con espressione" as part of tempo.

m. 325, **J**: no tempo head.

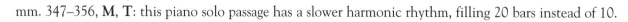

mm. 347–356, **M**, **T**: this piano solo passage has a slower harmonic rhythm, filling 20 bars instead of 10.

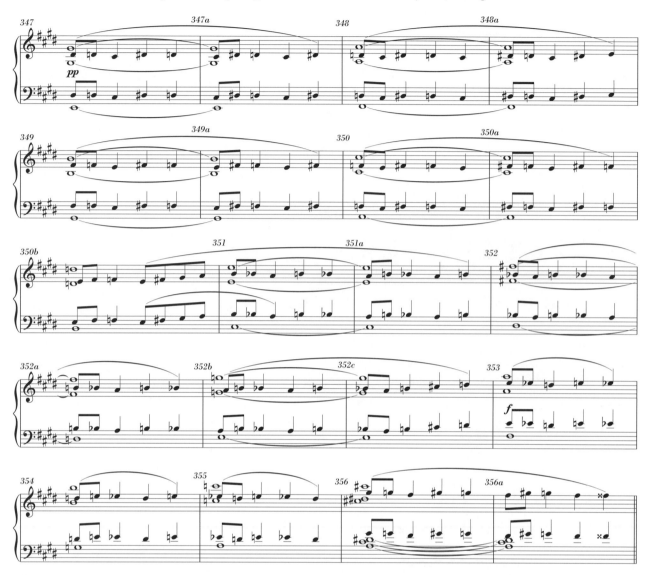

m. 382, **M, T**: 16 additional bars in the piano solo.

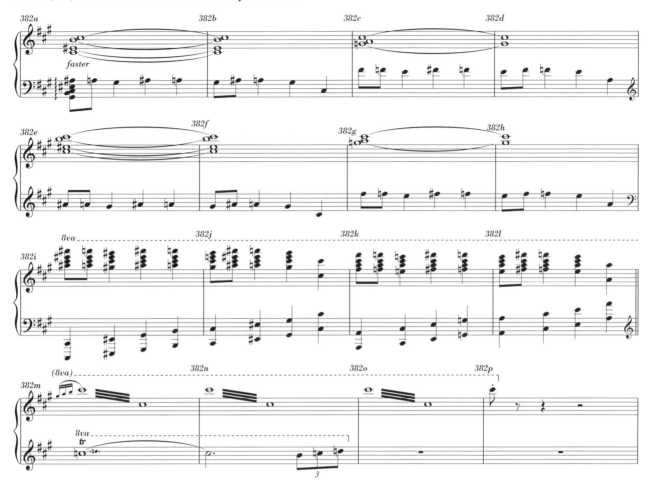

m. 386, **R^I, R^{II}**: cut from here to m. 415.

m. 414, **M**: 8 additional bars in piano solo.

m. 429, **J**: no tempo head.

m. 477, **J**: no *accel.* marking in either part.

m. 481, **J**: no tempo head.

m. 486, **J**: no fermata on caesura. **R**^{I}, **R**^{II}: no 32nd notes in orchestra, beat 4; cut from here to m. 501.

m. 487, **J**: tempo head **Grandioso** (*slower*). **W** has **Grandioso** (*not too slow*).

GEORGE GERSHWIN
RHAPSODY IN BLUE
2 PIANOS, 4 HANDS

Rhapsody in Blue
for Piano and Orchestra
(1924)

George Gershwin

N.B. Optional Cuts: A to B, C to D, E to F, G to H.

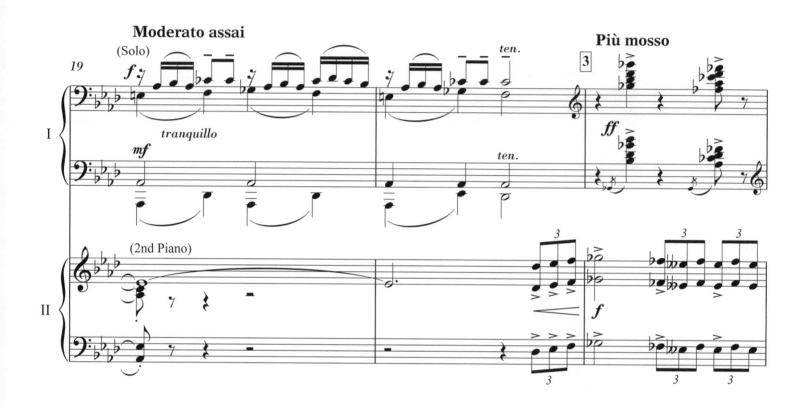

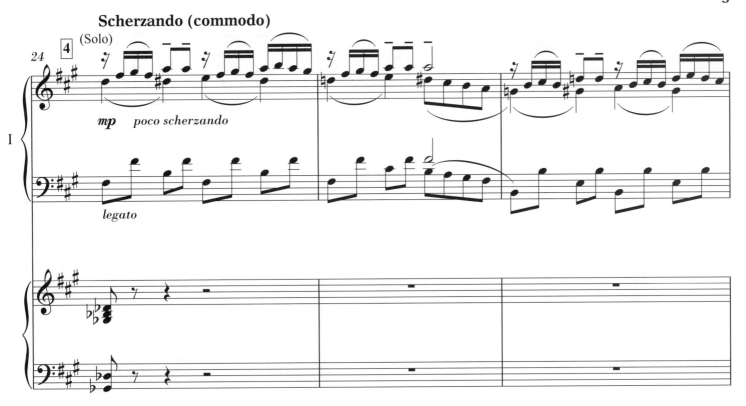

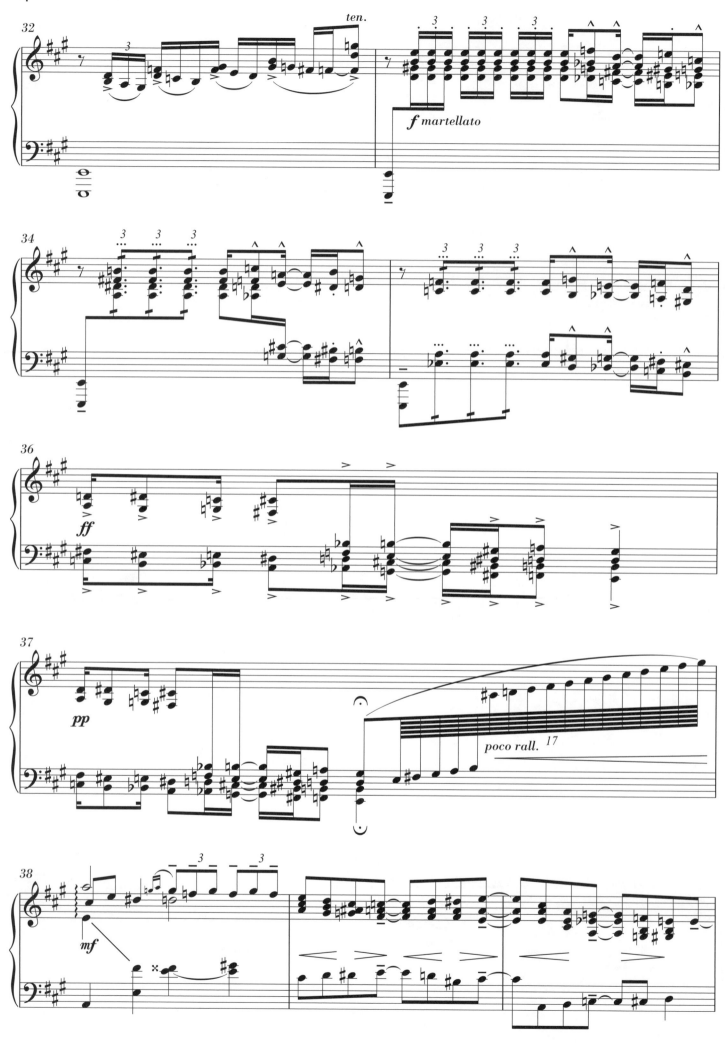

6 **Tempo giusto**

14

Meno mosso e poco scherzando
(Slower and marked)

GEORGE GERSHWIN
RHAPSODY IN BLUE
2 PIANOS, 4 HANDS

Edited by Brendan Fox

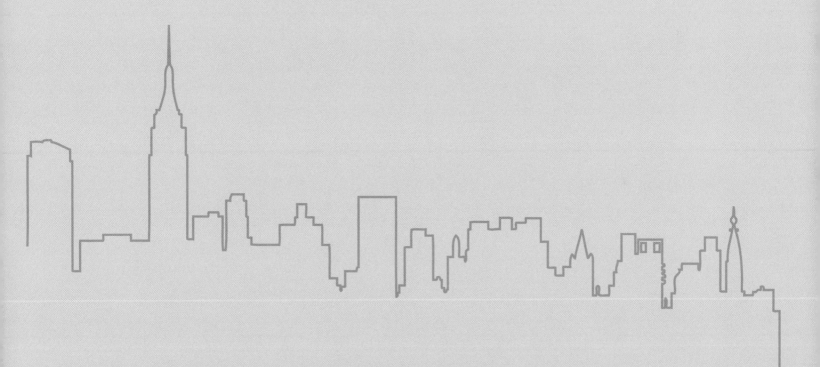

GERSHWIN® and GEORGE GERSHWIN®
are registered trademarks of Gershwin Enterprises

ISBN 978-1-5400-4027-5

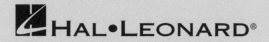

Contact us:
Hal Leonard
7777 West Bluemound Road
Milwaukee, WI 53213
Email: info@halleonard.com

In Europe, contact:
Hal Leonard Europe Limited
42 Wigmore Street
Marylebone, London, W1U 2RN
Email: info@halleonardeurope.com

In Australia, contact:
Hal Leonard Australia Pty. Ltd.
4 Lentara Court
Cheltenham, Victoria, 3192 Australia
Email: info@halleonard.com.au

Rhapsody in Blue
for Piano and Orchestra
(1924)

George Gershwin

Molto moderato (♩ = 80)

N.B. Optional Cuts: A to B, C to D, E to F, G to H.

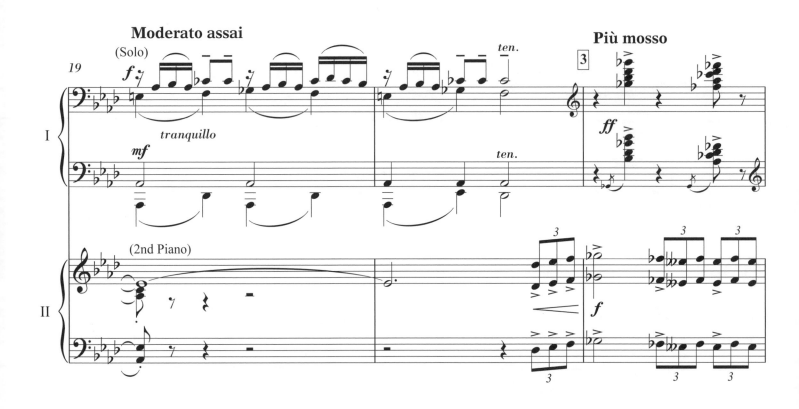

Scherzando (commodo)

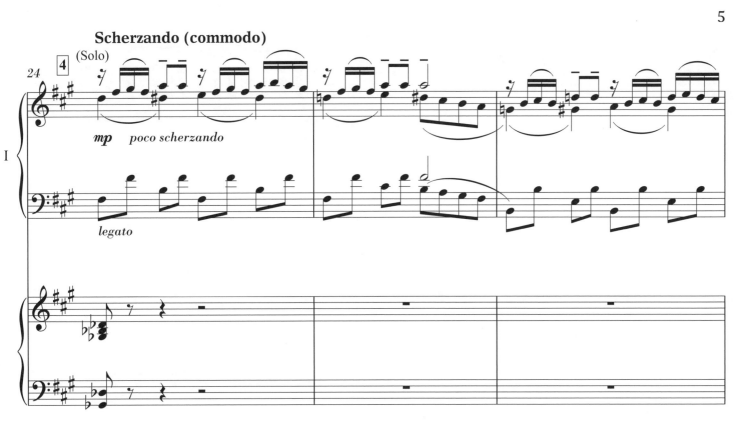

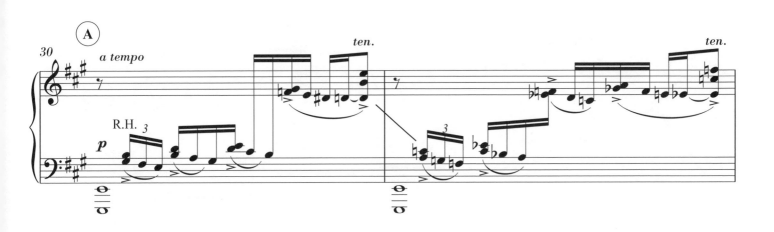

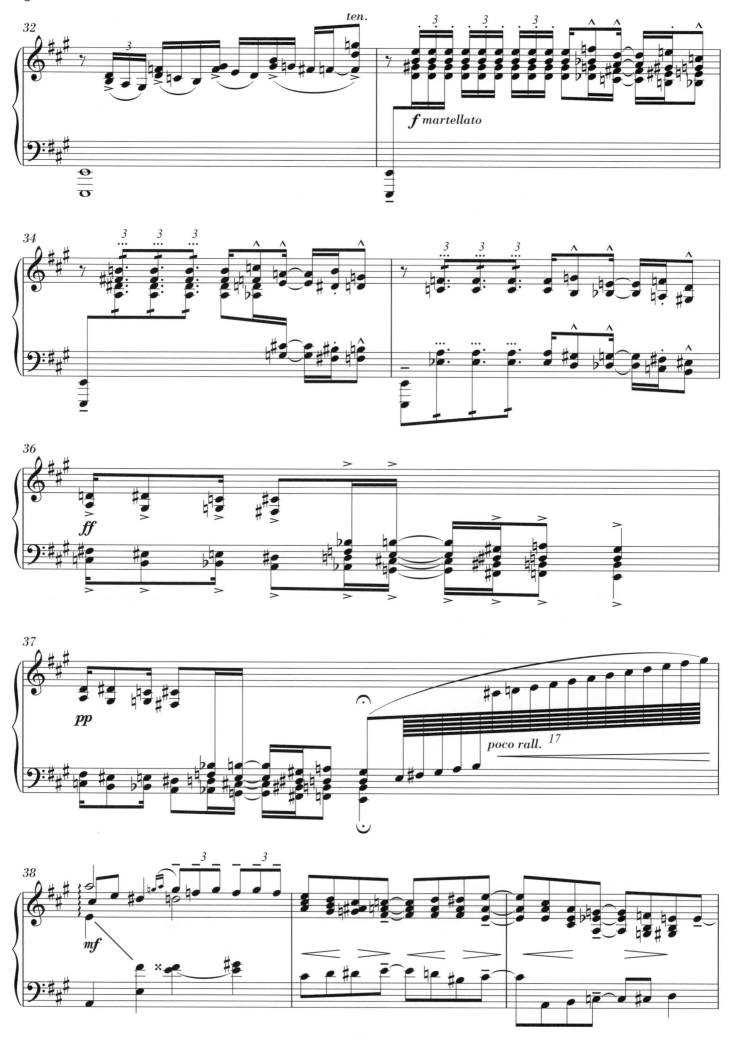

6 Tempo giusto

18

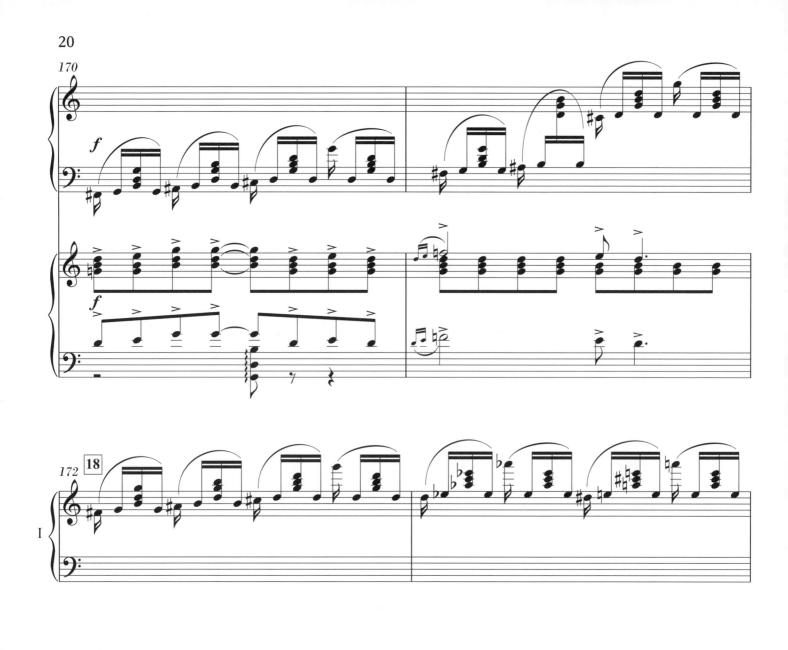

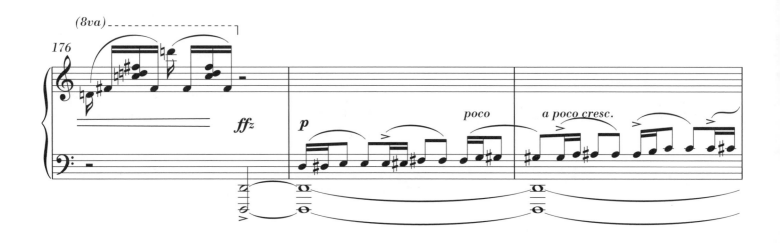

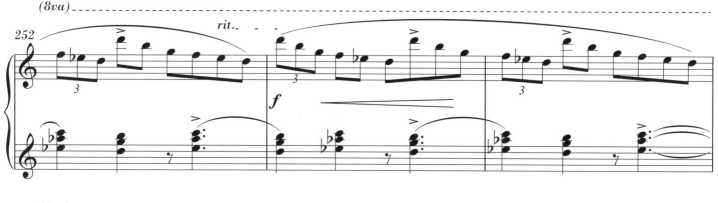

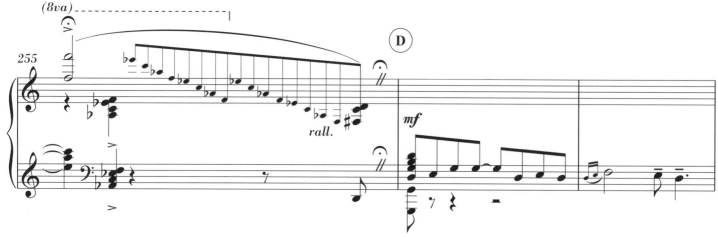

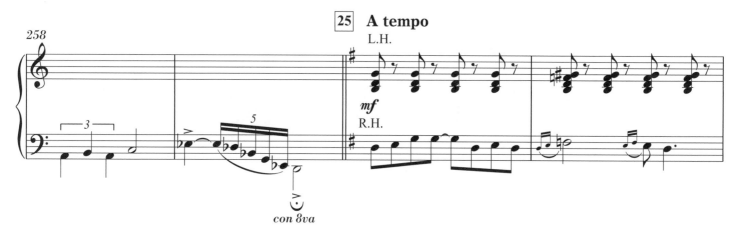

Andantino moderato con espressione

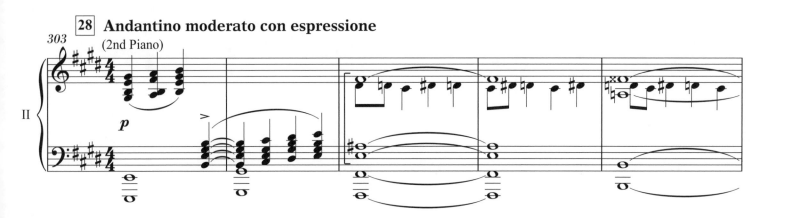

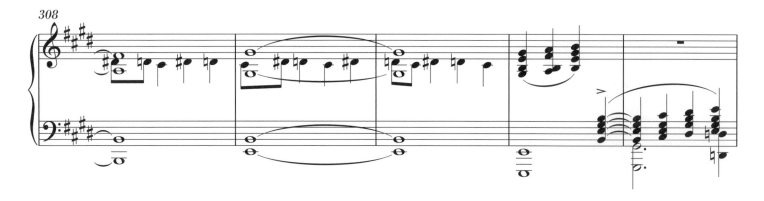

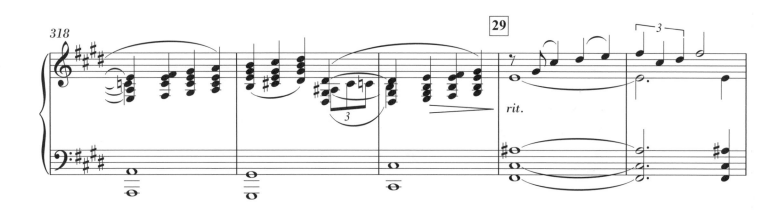

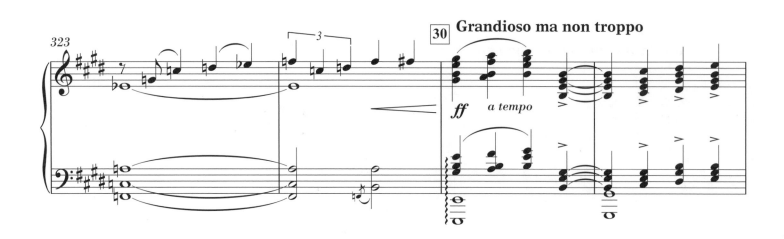

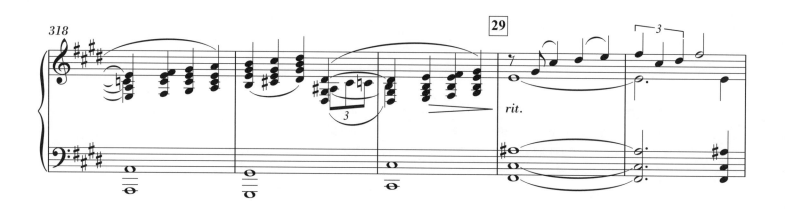

8va

441

trem. ad lib.

445

36 **Molto stentando**

449

ff

simile

ff